Daily Devotions for the Pastor's Wife

By the Executive Team of Pastors Wives Arise Network International (PWANI)

Daily Devotions for the Pastor's Wife by PWANI

Description

This collection of daily devotionals is written by pastors' wives, for pastors' wives with the sincere goal to bring encouragement to women who labor tirelessly for the Lord with their husbands. The devotionals focus on encouraging and strengthening the pastor's wife in her calling, self-care, raising of children, work in the ministry and most importantly, her relationship with God. Each contains key verses, prayers, and space to journal thoughts and reflections. You can spend a day or a week on a single devotion, depending on God's leading. Whatever the case, in each devotion, you'll find the voice of a woman with whom you can identify—and you can find comfort in knowing that she has also written in hopes of identifying with you.

Daily Devotions for the Pastor's Wife

By the Executive Team of Pastors Wives Arise Network International (PWANI)

Rev. Dr. Mercy Forlu
Dr. Elizabeth Fondong
Mrs. Danyel Forlu
Pastor Angie Millar
Rev. Lenita Reeves

*Purpose*House
Publishing

PurposeHouse Publishing
Edited and compiled by Pastor Lenita Reeves
Copyright © 2018

PurposeHouse Publishing, Columbia, Maryland
Copyright © 2018 PurposeHouse Publishing. All rights reserved.
Published 2018

Cover design by PurposeHouse Publishing, all rights reserved

No part of this publication may be reproduced or distributed in any form or by any means, or stored in a database or retrieval system, without the prior written permission of the publisher. Email requests for permission to ministeringpurpose@gmail.com.

Unless otherwise indicated, all scriptural quotations are from the King James Version of the Bible, which is in the public domain.

Scripture from Amplified Bible (AMP, Copyright © 1987 by the Lockman Foundation. (www.Lockman.org)

Scripture from the Living Bible (TLB), copyright © 1971 by Tyndale House Foundation, Used by permission of Tyndale House Publishers Inc., Carol Stream, Illinois 60188. All rights reserved.

Scripture from the New International Version (NIV), Copyright © 1973, 1978, 1984 by Biblica

Scripture from New King James Version (NKJV), Copyright © 1982 by Thomas Nelson, Inc., All rights reserved

Scripture from the New Life Version (NLV), Copyright © 1969 by Christian Literature International

Scripture from the New Living Translation (NLT), Copyright © 1996, 2004 by Tyndale Charitable Trust

Other titles from PurposeHouse publishing include:
I Love Me: 31 Daily Confessions to Restore Godly Confidence and Build Faith by Helena Barnes. For more information on PurposeHouse Publishing, visit www.publishing.purposehouse.net.

Connect With Us

For more information on Pastors Wives Arise Network International (PWANI), visit www.pastorswivesarise.com.

Dedication

This collection of devotions is dedicated to every wife of a minister, pastor, bishop or otherwise classified servant of God. Thank you for all that you do—sometimes without recognition or appreciation. Arise and shine for your light has come.

Contents

Introduction 9
There's healing for hurting. 15
Nothing but *the blood* can completely restore us. 19
You are not invisible. 21
The pastor's wife's outfit is love. 23
You have to choose the "good part." 25
Mother, where are you and where are your children? 29
Great is your heritage. 33
Find the balance. 35
The pastor's wife's perfume is joy. 37
Timing is everything. 39
God has a plan. 41
Clean me out. 43
You were chosen by God. 45
The pastor's wife's pocket book is patience. 47
There is no "one size fits all." 49
Who counsels you? 51
Is there a sister's keeper? 53
The pastor's wife's hairdo is wisdom. 57
Our children are nations. 59
Everyone needs compassion. 61
The pastor's wife's shoes are peace. 63

Daily Devotions for the Pastor's Wife by PWANI

You have the power to swim gracefully—even in a fishbowl. 65
Do not defile the priesthood. 67
Celebrate your uniqueness. 69
You're the only animal in this zoo. 73
You've been enlisted. 77
There's grace to run the race. 79
About the Authors 81

Introduction

The office of a pastor's wife is a great one with very important responsibilities. Many pastors' wives will tell you that they did not fight to take this office; they just found themselves in it. For many of us, we accept it with all our hearts, and depend on God for the grace to do our assignments to the finish.

I see it as a calling, and a privilege to be a pastor's wife. The job can be delicate, and challenging, as you have to care for the Lord's anointed (your husband), your children (who are also the Lord's anointed), relatives, and God's people whom you both lead. Notwithstanding, God divinely empowers the pastor's wife, and gives her spiritual insight and understanding of what it takes to be a good pastor's wife.

Every pastor's wife can determine to increase and strengthen her spiritual muscles and be up to the task; and increase in spiritual height and momentum; steadily going higher and higher, never giving up, until God's purpose is accomplished.

This is the reason for the Pastors' Wives Arise Network International (PWANI). This network seeks to connect with one another, and be a support to our fellow sisters in this same office. To provide mentorship and counseling as need be, under the leadership of the Holy Spirit, and abiding in the Word of God. Many pastors' wives go through common challenges, and a testimony of how one overcame a certain challenge, may be the light that will break forth to give a breakthrough to another pastor's wife encountering a similar challenge.

Dear pastors' wife, you have done much, but you have not yet reached the finishing mark; do not be satisfied with where you are, and with what you have done so far. There is still much to do.

There are still more:

- territories to conquer;
- souls to be saved;
- hungry mouths to be fed;
- poor and needy to be help;
- critical decisions for you and your husband to take;
- things for your children to accomplish;
- persons to be delivered from demonic chains;
- spiritual babies to fed;
- maybe, more trials and temptations to overcome;
- families to build;
- sons and daughters that must come to you; and
- nations to come to your light, and more kings to the brightness of your light.

Pastors' wives, *"Arise, shine, for your light has come, and the glory of the Lord has risen upon you. For the darkness shall cover the earth and deep darkness the peoples; but the Lord shall rise upon you, and His glory shall be seen upon you. The nations shall come to your light and kings to the brightness of your rising." (Isaiah 60:1-3)*

Arise to your next level of watching and praying. Arise and pray more for your husband, your children, and your generations to come. Do not give up. God is ready to give you wings and eyes like those of an eagle.

The days are evil. You need powerful wings to soar high like an eagle. You need the eyes of an eagle to be able to see the enemies of your husband, children, and ministry from afar off, and deal with them with the weapons of warfare that the Lord has given you.

Arise to your next level of commitment, devotedness, and service to the Lord Jesus Christ.

Arise so that you can be of help to any of the saints that may be fainting.

Arise and be the one to equip the next generation.

Arise and to accomplish your purpose and arrive your destiny.

Arise and be counted among the faithful.

Pastors' wives arise!

Rev. Dr. Mercy Forlu, a pastor's wife
President, PWANI

Daily Devotions for the Pastor's Wife

By the Executive Team of Pastors Wives Arise Network International (PWANI)

There's healing for hurting.

> *Fear thou not; for I am with thee: be not dismayed; for I am thy God: I will strengthen thee; yea, I will help thee; yea, I will uphold thee with the right hand of my righteousness. (Isaiah 41: 10, King James Version (KJV))*

In my early years as a pastor's wife, I was inexperienced. I learned mostly from observing the elderly Christians in church. I was a young Christian--and a young pastor's wife--when I received the first blow of offense from one of the members. I was not ready for such a blow. I expected every Christian in church to be well-behaved, sincerely loving God and the brethren. I was angry and hurt. I expressed my hurt to this believer; but it did not help. For many days, the sun went down on my anger and pain. I thought of what to do to get revenge; but arrived at nothing.

Then, I attended a conference where a pastor's wife was the speaker. Her topic was forgiveness. At the time, I couldn't imagine that God would set up such a meeting only to teach me about forgiveness and how he can heal my pain. As I listened to this lady, I felt that God was not being fair to me. My thought was that God should sympathize with me, rather than emphasize that I should forgive. My thoughts began to change when the speaker said: "If you are not willing to forgive, be honest and tell God....ask him to help you to be willing to forgive." She went on, "Or, if you are willing to forgive, but you are not able to forgive, ask the Holy Spirit to sow the seed of forgiveness in your heart." I had never heard anything like that. I decided to ask the Holy Spirit to sow that seed of forgiveness in me. At that moment, my thoughts concerning the offender changed. Then, I said, "Lord, I forgive and I let go." This time it was with all my heart. There was a shift in my spirit. I felt peace and I felt light. A weight was lifted off me. I realized I just received healing for hurting.

As a pastor's wife, you may be falsely accused, gossiped about or ill-treated in various ways. Be not discouraged. The Lord says he will help you. The Lord helped me to forgive and be free. He can do the same for you. Ask God for help. Your hurt can disappear with the smooth touch of the Holy Spirit.

Key Verse: "But if ye forgive not men their trespasses, neither will your Father forgive your trespasses." (Matthew 6:15, KJV)

Prayer: Lord, may the seed of forgiveness be sown in my heart. Help me to release and forgive as you have forgiven me. In Jesus' name, I pray. Amen.

Rev. Dr. Mercy Forlu.

Daily Devotions for the Pastor's Wife by PWANI

Nothing but *the blood* can completely restore us.

> *For you know that God paid a ransom to save you from the empty life you inherited from your ancestors. And it was not paid with mere gold or silver, which lose their value. It was the precious blood of Christ, the sinless, spotless Lamb of God. (1 Peter 1:18-19, New Living Translation (NLT))*

Years ago, I read a story about the value and daily use of clay pots during the first century. They were typically made of clay from the Jordan River and were used to carry water and preserve food. Most homes only had a few of these pots; therefore, if one broke or cracked, repairing it was vital. Unfortunately, many of the techniques used to repair the pots failed or left extreme blemishes on the outside. The pots were never completely whole again.

One day, a potter decided to try something different. He took clay from the Jordan River and mixed it with the blood from a tick that he had removed from a lamb. When the clay and blood mixture was applied to the cracked vessel, and then dried in the sun, the vessel became whole again and the blemish vanished. Hallelujah. We have all been a broken vessel at some point in our life; but, when the blood of the Lamb is applied and we are allowed to bask in the Son--we are repaired, made whole, and without blemish. Nothing but the blood of the Lamb, Jesus, can save us and make us whole again.

Prayer: Lord, I thank you for healing, restoring, cleansing, and saving me with your precious blood. I give you praise. In Jesus' name, I pray. Amen.

Pastor Angie Millar

You are not invisible.

> *For God is not unjust. He will not forget how hard you have worked for him and how you have shown your love to him by caring for other believers, as you still do.* (Hebrews 6:10, NLT)

You may wonder if anyone sees the sacrifices you are making, the countless hours you put in working at the church, supporting your husband, praying for the congregants, and ministering to the lost. The good news is your father in heaven sees your sacrifices and, in Colossians 3:23, he commands us to work diligently--as if we're working for the Lord rather than people. Take joy in working for the kingdom of heaven. God has placed you where you are for a reason and has called you to be the backbone of the church in which he placed you. He sees you. Don't become discouraged when you don't get the recognition you feel you deserve for all your hard work. Your rewards await you in heaven.

Key Verse: "Work willingly at whatever you do, as though you were working for the Lord rather than for people." (Colossians 3:23, NLT)

Prayer: Lord, help me to focus on you as I work diligently. Help me to remember always, that you will not forget what I do for your kingdom. In Jesus' name, I pray. Amen.

Mrs. Danyel Forlu

Daily Devotions for the Pastor's Wife by PWANI

The pastor's wife's outfit is love.

And all of you who have been united with Christ in baptism have put on Christ, like putting on new clothes. (Galatians 3:27, NLT)

I remember looking at a magazine when I had just gotten married and enjoying all the beautiful outfits that were specially designed for pastors' wives. They were so unique and full of glamor and style. Unknown to me, the job of a pastor's wife required much more than pretty outfits. There is a much more distinguished outfit for you, pastor's wife. It is a heavenly outfit, designed by God himself whose durability is eternal. It is a royal outfit that increases in shine with every use. It is one that you never have to take off--God's own outfit called love. God has poured his love into your heart by the Holy Spirit (Romans 5:5), freely giving of himself by the Spirit. You have freely received of God's love, so freely give of his love.

Through Holy Spirit, you have been empowered to love people the same way that God has loved you (John 15:12). If you constantly let Christ make his home in your heart, your roots will grow down into God's love and keep you strong. (Ephesians 3:17) Love is the outfit that is attractive to our heavenly husband, God and makes him at home in our hearts. Love is the outfit that distinguishes you as a virtuous woman, a wife whose husband safely trusts her and has no need of spoil. (Proverbs 31:11)

Key Verse: Anyone who does not love does not know God, because God is love. (1 John 4:8, ESV)

Prayer: Lord God, today I receive power to comprehend with all that saints what is the length and the width and height and the depth of God's love. In Jesus' name, I pray. Amen.

Dr. Elizabeth Fondong

You have to choose the "good part."

> But the Lord replied to her, "Martha, Martha, you are worried and bothered and anxious about so many things; [42] but only one thing is necessary, for Mary has chosen the good part [that which is to her advantage], which will not be taken away from her." (Luke 10:41-42, AMP)

Several years ago, I heard Kay Warren, wife of Rick Warren say, "You have to take care of yourself; nobody else in the ministry is going to do that for you—not even your husband." She was speaking about the importance of self-care for women in ministry. At the time, I was so "green" in ministry I couldn't fully appreciate the value of the words she was speaking. Now, after several years in senior leadership, I can truly testify that what she said is so true.

Not only do you have to take care of yourself but you also have to choose what's to your advantage when it comes to your health and mental well-being. If solitude energizes you, you have to build it into your schedule. If interaction with people energizes you, you have to build it into your schedule. Find creative ways to get enough water, take your vitamins, and nap every now and then. There's even an app that reminds you to drink water.

You have to be intentional about taking care of your body, soul, and spirit. You have to be intentional about resting and getting enough sleep. These things may seem trivial; but, if you are like me, a choleric, *Type-A* workaholic, you know the danger of inadequate time to rest your mind, body, and spirit.

Jesus warned Martha about this danger. He told her to learn a lesson from her sister, Mary, who had exhibited wisdom and intentionality. Mary chose the thing that was going to reinvigorate her spirit, soul, and body--sitting at the feet of Jesus. In other words, Mary chose *self-care*, but Martha chose to care for many other things. Mary chose the "good part," will you? Today, be sure to find time for yourself. Completely disconnect from social media, texts, and alerts so you can fully relax and just enjoy time in the presence of God. It is the only way you can be the best version of yourself when everyone begins to pull on you.

Prayer: Father, teach me to prioritize that "good part" that will bring balance, rest, and energy to my soul. Help me to choose to sit at your feet. Help me to develop a healthy rhythm of work and self-care. In Jesus' name, I pray. Amen.

Rev. Lenita Reeves

Daily Devotions for the Pastor's Wife by PWANI

Mother, where are you, and where are your children?

Train up a child in the way he should go: and when he is old, he will not depart from it. (Proverbs 22: 6, KJV)

As I read 1 Samuel chapters two and three, I understand that Eli was a priest chosen by God; and, he had sons who sinned so grievously against God that God had to bring severe judgment upon the whole family. God had indeed promised that He would bless Eli, and his seed would stand before Him to serve Him for generations.

And even though the sons of Eli began to provoke God to anger through their immorality and greed, there is no record of intercession for these children. Where was their mother? Did she bother to know where her children were, and what they were doing? Did she play any role in training her children in the ways of God? Was she just too preoccupied with her jobs or businesses or ministering to other people and neglecting her own children?

God says he is looking for just one person to stand in the gap for the sinner. If Eli's wife was a woman of prayer, she could have at least interceded for her children and her household. God could have changed the verdict because he is a merciful God. Instead, all her sons died in one day. God's judgment was established and they were cut off from the priesthood forever.

Mother, plant your children in the house of the Lord, by intentionally building them up with the word of God and watching over them with your prayers. They will not bring you sorrow but will flourish spiritually, physically, financially and in a very good way in the courts of our God.

Key Verse: "Those that be planted in the house of the Lord shall flourish in the courts of our God." (Psalms 92:13, KJV)

Prayer: Lord, help me to focus on the godly upbringing of my children, so I can be of great influence in shaping their destinies. In Jesus' name, I pray. Amen.

Rev. Dr. Mercy Forlu.

Daily Devotions for the Pastor's Wife by PWANI

Great is your heritage.

Behold, children are a heritage from the LORD, the fruit of the womb a reward. (Psalm 127:3 (ESV))

Heritage is defined as "property that descends to an heir" or "something possessed as a result of one's natural situation or birth." God considers us his heirs. So, he has given us children as an inheritance just as priceless antiques, jewelry, valuable property, and irreplaceable works of art are handed down through generations. God has given us children as extraordinary and precious beings that require special handling and consideration. He trusts us with the care that they need to grow, flourish, and become the adults who will in turn, nurture the inheritance that is entrusted to them. God trusts us to recognize the value in our children and those in our care today. He empowers us with the wisdom, patience, and virtue we need to assure that not only are their needs met but also that they receive the best care and nurturing possible. He wants us to make him proud as we prepare our children to become role models, leaders, and parents themselves.

How blessed to know that the great, *Almighty God* chose you, yes you, to be a part of shaping history. For, as mothers raising *his* children, that is what we are called and instructed to do. You've got this woman of God!

Prayer: Lord, thank you for choosing me to raise the next generation of kingdom warriors, evangelists, intercessors, worship leaders and so much more for generations to come. In Jesus' name, I pray. Amen.

Pastor Angie Millar

Find the balance.

> *But those who won't care for their relatives, especially those in their own household, have denied the true faith. Such people are worse than unbelievers. (1 Timothy 5:8, NLT)*

My husband and I are a young couple with young children. I sometimes have to step back in ministry to allow my husband to fulfill his calling while I take care of the kids. When we had our first son, it was relatively easy for both of us to continue ministry work. But when our second son was born our oldest was only 13 months. It became difficult for both of us to be active in ministry. I remember us discussing the "good" problem we had encountered: both of us having ministry responsibilities but one of us needing to take care of our sons. The easy compromise was for my husband to continue what he needed to do and for me to do to support him. I was able to assist behind the scenes, doing work that I could take care of from home. Now, we have four children: ages seven, six, three, and seven months. We are busier than ever, and my husband and I continue to support each other. It's a team effort. When needed, he takes care of our children while I'm serving in ministry or vice versa.

Find the balance. Have an open and honest dialogue with your husband about the very important issue of home and ministry balance. Take care of your family first.

Prayer: Lord, help me to find the important balance between serving my family and serving in the ministry. In Jesus' name, I pray. Amen.

Mrs. Danyel Forlu

The pastor's wife's perfume is joy.

With joy you will draw from the wells of salvation. (Isaiah 12:3, NKJV)

Perfume has benefits for the one who wears it as well as those around them. Some of the benefits of perfume are it enhances mood, boosts confidence, triggers memories and makes the wearer more attractive.

Joy is your heavenly perfume. You put it on and you draw from the wells of God's salvation. You draw strength from God and you attract strength (goodness) from others. When we neglect this fruit of the spirit, we are unconsciously drawing and tapping into our pain, regrets, and failures and, the result is weakness and defeat.

However, as a pastor's wife, focus on Zephaniah 3:17 which says, "The Lord your God is with you, the mighty warrior who saves. He will take great delight in you; in his love, he will no longer rebuke you, but will rejoice over you with singing." The Scripture is reminding you that the Lord your God is with you. You are not alone. Fix your thoughts on the mighty warrior who saves. Gaze at God who rejoices over you with joy, who rejoices over you with shouts of joy.

Prayer: Lord, grant me to know that joy is a choice based on seeing you rejoicing over me with singing. I choose to rejoice always. In Jesus' name, I pray. Amen.

Dr. Elizabeth Fondong

Timing is everything.

> *A word spoken at the right time is like fruit of gold set in silver.* (Proverbs 25:11, NLV)
> *When she speaks, her words are wise, and she gives instructions with kindness.* (Proverbs 31:26, NLT)

Undoubtedly, there will be times when you feel bombarded by the needs, requests, and demands of the people you serve: your husband, children, employer, and church members all place demands on you. Sometimes, church members bring a problem or an important piece of information when you have just had to resolve a heated conflict, or are preparing to speak. The information may truly be important but delivered at the wrong time. Timing is the reason you are unable to process the information or give it proper attention.

The same is true when dealing with your husband. Timing is everything, especially when you have to communicate about sensitive issues. Whether it's about church or the children, there will always be times when you see things differently than your husband. Be sure to evaluate the timing. Ask yourself whether it is the right time to address the issue and pray for grace and wisdom to speak at the right time. The issue may be burning in your heart: you may want to talk immediately and "put everything on the table." However, your husband may be bombarded with other issues. Be still. Wait. The right time will come. God will give you grace.

A change in timing doesn't mean God is unable to work in the situation. Sometimes, he wants us to defer discussing a matter. He wants us to mature and exercise patience so the right result can manifest.

Key Verse: The discretion of a man deferreth his anger; and it is his glory to pass over a transgression. (Proverbs 19:11, KJV)

Prayer: Lord, help me to speak at the right time. Let wisdom be upon my lips and give me influence with my husband. In Jesus' name, I pray. Amen.

Rev. Lenita Reeves

God has a plan.

> *For I know the thoughts that I think towards you, saith the Lord, thoughts of peace and not of evil, to give you an expected end. (Jeremiah 29: 11, KJV)*

Sometimes you face situations that keep you wondering if ends will ever meet. Difficulties mount up and you can hardly tell where they are coming from and where they are going. Some call it the wind of life. Some call it life challenges. Some call it trials and some say it's adversity. Whatever it is, God's handmaiden, remember you are God's own. He has a plan for you and your family. And he can never fail. Let every man be a liar, but God cannot lie. Surely, he has spoken his word over your life. He may not repeat it over and over to you. If he has spoken, it is done. The ways of God are unsearchable. He often comes in directions we do not imagine.

Peter saw Jesus walking on the water. He stepped out in faith on the Lord's word, "Come." He was doing this for his first time. The Lord knew that Peter was not going to make it without the sinking experience. The Lord had a plan to deliver him from sinking. Peter did not foresee the wind and the storm coming, but the Lord saw it ahead of time. Woman of God, whatever you are going through right now, (even if it is your own fault) God saw it ahead of time. And he has a plan to help you. He will never leave you nor forsake you. Trust in the Lord with all your heart and lean not on your own understanding. He loves you. He is reaching out to you now to make all things work for your good and His glory.

Key Verse: "And the Lord, He it is that doth go before thee; He will be with thee; He will not fail thee, neither forsake thee: fear not, neither be dismayed." (Deuteronomy 31:8, KJV)

Prayer: Lord, I thank you for your plans for my life. I accept it, I receive your help and, I receive grace for victory and a breakthrough. In Jesus' name, I pray. Amen.

Rev. Dr. Mercy Forlu.

Daily Devotions for the Pastor's Wife by PWANI

Clean me out.

Create in me a clean heart, O God, and renew a right spirit within me. (Psalm 51:10, KJV)

Every now and again, we have to clean out our refrigerators and closets because over time, they can easily become filled with things that are expired (turning into the makings of penicillin), no longer needed, or just don't fit our needs anymore. We sometimes hang onto clothes that we have outgrown. The same thing goes for our hearts. There is a reason that it is necessary to ask God to create in us a clean heart and renew a right spirit within us--daily. Our hearts can easily become cluttered with old hurts, past pains, and unresolved matters that if we are not careful, could cause us to have a heart of stone and cause us to make decisions that are not in line with the will of God. Scripture also instructs us to take every thought captive; therefore, we must clean our hearts of destructive thoughts. Any thought that does not bring glory to God is untruthful and must be removed. If we allow them to remain it can damage our relationship with others, or worse, it could ruin our witness as Christians, as God's handmaidens. Make no mistake. We are human. We are made of flesh. As a result, we have to be constantly on guard that our hearts are not corrupt with things that hinder us from living a blessed and fulfilling life.

Prayer: Lord, create in me a clean heart. Show me what needs to be removed or no longer fits in the design you have for me. Replace the unneeded with useful things. In Jesus' name, I pray. Amen.

Pastor Angie Millar

You were chosen by God.

> *Have I not commanded you? Be strong and courageous. Do not be afraid; do not be discouraged, for the LORD your God will be with you wherever you go. (Joshua 1:9, NIV)*

It may feel like you are in the trenches with no light in sight, no one to help, and no one to encourage you to keep going. But, you can make it. You will make it! God is with you. He sees every tear you have shed and every sacrifice you have made. God chose you, called you to be a pastor's wife and he never makes a mistake. Even if you feel like you are not qualified, God has not made a mistake.

I have to remind myself that *God* called me to marry my husband and be his helpmate. There are millions of women in the world, but God chose me--hand-selected me--to serve alongside my husband. No other woman can fill the role of Mrs. Ryan Forlu; and because God chose me, I know He will be with me and guide me. Be strong. Be courageous. God is with you. He will never leave you.

Prayer: Lord, help me to be strong and courageous. Give me the confidence and boldness I need to stand alongside my husband. **In Jesus' name, I pray.** Amen.

Mrs. Danyel Forlu

Daily Devotions for the Pastor's Wife by PWANI

The pastor's wife's pocket book is patience.

But let patience have her perfect work, that you may be perfect and complete, lacking nothing. (James 1:4, NKJV)

Imagine with me, the embarrassment of standing in front of a cashier ready to make a payment and your credit card is declined. The first thought is, "what happened to my money." No one enjoys being in a position of lack, feeling incomplete or inadequate.

Patience is a fruit of the Spirit assigned by God to do a perfect work in us. Patience has a goal of perfecting and completing you. What makes us impatient is the inability to see the end. You can focus so intently on the now that you lose sight of the big picture for the future. Ecclesiastes 7:8 says, "The end of something is better than its beginning. Patience is better than pride." Take heart woman of God, the end of your ministry will be better than the beginning. Patience is necessary. Just as you will not step out of the house, on a journey without your pocketbook, because it holds all your essential documents don't attempt this journey without patience by your side.

Key Verse: You, too, must be patient. Take courage, for the coming of the Lord is near. (James 5:8, NLT)

Prayer: Lord, grant me to understand that you are not slow to fulfill your promises as some count slowness, but are patient toward me, not wishing that any should perish, but that all should reach repentance. (2 Peter 3:9) In Jesus' name, I pray. Amen.

Dr. Elizabeth Fondong

There is no "one size fits all."

> *For we are His workmanship [His own master work, a work of art], created in Christ Jesus [reborn from above—spiritually transformed, renewed, ready to be used] for good works, which God prepared [for us] beforehand [taking paths which He set], so that we would walk in them [living the good life which He prearranged and made ready for us]. (Ephesians 2:10, Amplified Bible (AMP))*

When you find a "One Size Fits All Garment" in the store, it's usually because the designer has deemed it big enough to fit almost all body types and sizes. Pastors' wives come in all body types and sizes, and the role of a pastor's wife is not "one size fits all." It's not cookie-cutter; meaning, there's not a single pattern for the role of a pastor's wife. Some pastors' wives have the sole assignment of serving their husbands and children while others have been endowed with five-fold gifts, having the additional responsibility to help govern the affairs of the church.

Often, pastors' wives are confronted with varied responsibilities and competing priorities. But you don't have to do it all. Focus on finding out what God requires of you as an individual believer, endowed with gifts and predestined for good works.

In the end, we will all stand before God and give an account for the works that he preordained that we should work on the earth. We won't stand alongside our husbands on that day, for they neither marry nor are given in marriage in heaven. (Matthew 22:30) We will stand alone; giving account for the gifts that God placed in us—gifts that he endowed us with for a particular assignment during our time on earth. Before we were wives, we were—and still are—God's workmanship created in Christ Jesus for good works that we should walk in them. Each pastor's wife brings something unique to her marriage and ministry. Discover who you are in him. Discover the cut of your cloth; because, when it comes to calling, there is no "one size fits all."

Key Verse: Each one's work will be clearly shown [for what it is]; for the day [of judgment] will disclose it, because it is to be revealed with fire, and the fire will test the quality and character and worth of each person's work. (1 Corinthians 3:13, AMP)

Prayer: Lord, help me to discover my gifts, passions, and assignment on earth so that I can stand boldly before you on the Day of Judgment and hear, "well done." In Jesus' name, I pray. Amen.

Rev. Lenita Reeves

Who counsels you?

> *Blessed is the man that walketh not in the counsel of the ungodly, nor standeth in the way of sinners, nor sitteth in the seat of the scornful. But his delight is in the law of the Lord; and in His law doth he meditate day and night. (Psalms 1:1- 2, KJV)*

Who counsels you *Woman of God*? Where do you take your concerns? As pastors' wives, we need a lot of wisdom. It is often said that the pastor's wife does not have friends, she does not know with whom to share her deepest worries. Sometimes she cannot even share her concerns with her husband, because her husband could be the reason for the problems in question. So to whom can she go? If she dares to open her mouth to any member of the congregation, no matter how spiritual they may appear to be, she might be opening a great chapter for ridicule and slander. Some people do not see pastors' wives as people who could have their own problems; yet pastors' wives need help, just like every other human being. So why are they often ill spoken of and ridiculed? God alone knows.

The word of God says, "Be still and know that I am God...." When tough times come, be still. When you do know who to talk to—be still. Just be still. If you can't be still, ask for the grace to be still. While you are still, stay in prayer; cry out to God. If you have to, worship Him; if you have to, dance a faith dance of victory; if you have to, ask in prayer; if you have to, make decrees and declarations. In the presence of God, before you know it, he will instruct you and teach you in the way you should go, and he will guide you with his eye. If he chooses so, God will lead you to someone godly you should talk to; or give you the solution in his presence as you wait on Him.

Key Verse: "I will instruct thee and teach thee in the way which thou shalt go: I will guide thee with mine eye." (Psalms 32:8, KJV)

Prayer: Lord show me your way and teach me your paths. Let me never be ashamed and let not mine enemies triumph over me. In Jesus' name, I pray. Amen.

Rev. Dr. Mercy Forlu.

Is there a sister's keeper?

> *And the Lord said unto Cain, Where is Abel thy brother? And he said, I know not: Am I my brother's keeper? (Genesis 4:9, KJV)*

The phrase, "No man is an island" is a quotation from the English, metaphysical poet John Donne and it appears in *Devotions Upon Emergent Occasions and Seuerall Steps in my Sickness - Meditation XVII*, 1624. (Gray 2018) The full poem follows:

> No man is an island entire of itself; every man is a piece of the continent, a part of the main; if a clod be washed away by the sea, Europe is the less, as well as if a promontory were, as well as any manner of thy friends or of thine own were; any man's death diminishes me, because I am involved in mankind. And therefore never send to know for whom the bell tolls; it tolls for thee.

In his poem, Donne expressed what Scripture had already articulated: we are members of each other. We are members of Christ's body. No body part can survive in isolation. Eyes cannot function without a head. Fingers cannot operate without an arm.

Yet, somehow, pastors' wives end up being the most isolated people in the church. They often feel trapped. They are keenly aware of their need for fellowship but remain isolated for fear of betrayal, insincerity, or gossip. They are left asking, "Is there a sister's keeper? Who will be my confidant? Who will encourage me? Who will listen to me?"

It is true that some women will never be trustworthy enough to merit the precious friendship of a pastor's wife. However, it is also true that mature, loving pastors' wives can be a nurturing source of comfort. God encourages you today to refuse isolation and nurture a healthy relationship with a mature sister in Christ. To have friends, we must also be friendly. Today, decide to be a sister's keeper and reverse the negative trend of isolation affecting pastors' wives. Call a pastor's wife today. Pray for her. Encourage her. In the end, you will reap the love that you sow.

Key Verse: A man who has friends must himself be friendly, But there is a friend who sticks closer than a brother. (Proverbs 18:24, NKJV)

Prayer: Lord, help me to be an example of godly sisterhood. I will not isolate myself. I will sow friendliness so I can also reap friendliness. I choose to sow love so I can also reap love. In Jesus' name, I pray. Amen.

Rev. Lenita Reeves

The pastor's wife's hairdo is wisdom.

> Wisdom *will reward you with a* crown *of honor and glory."*
> *(Proverbs 4:9, ERV)*

The hair of a woman is often seen as a reflection of her identity because it is both personal and public. Think about the time, money and emotion that you put into your hair and its presentation. A bad hair day easily results in a bad day. For a pastor's wife, the high expectations from her husband, her congregation and community only add to her own personal struggles and insecurities around her hair. People place a lot of importance on hair and rightly so, for even Jesus himself took the time to number every hair on our heads (Luke 12:7).

But let's look at something that carries superior importance to God. Proverbs 4:7 says, "Wisdom is the principal thing; therefore get wisdom: and with all your getting get understanding." Wisdom makes the most of every opportunity. According to Ephesians 5:16, we should make the most of every opportunity to serve our husbands, children, and the body of Christ. It is an opportunity for greatness, for the servant is the greatest of all.

Wisdom from heaven is peace-loving, considerate, submissive, full of mercy and good fruit, and impartial and sincere. (James 1:5) Godly wisdom is displayed in your character and how you treat people. In contrast to worldly, educational wisdom, the wisdom of God is the manifestation of the presence of the all-wise God. Wisdom is displayed in our speech (Colossians 4:5-6); meaning, our conversation should always be full of grace and seasoned with salt so that we may know how to answer everyone.

Prayer: Lord, today I receive wisdom that comes from above, the wisdom to make the most of every opportunity, and the wisdom to answer correctly. In Jesus' name, I pray. Amen.

Dr. Elizabeth Fondong

Our children are nations.

> *And the Lord said unto her, two nations are in your womb, and two manner of people shall be separated from thy bowels; ...and the elder shall serve the younger. (Genesis 25:23, KJV)*

Rebecca, Isaac's wife, was pregnant and as the Bible says, she felt the children struggling within her. Being uncomfortable about it, she inquired from the Lord, and the Lord said, "Two nations are in your womb."

Woman of God, our children are nations. And God says that he has set us over these nations (our children) to root out from them and to pull down, destroy and throw down what God has not planted nor placed in them. We are also to build their lives with the word of God, to plant the word of God in them, and to plant them in the house of God. In our prayers, our conversations, counseling and daily walk with God, we intentionally add value to our lives and that of our children, towards uprooting that which is wrong, and instilling or sowing what is right in shaping their destinies for God's glory.

Key Verse: "See I have this day set thee over the nations and over the kingdoms, to root out, and to pull down, and to destroy, and to throw down, to build, and to plant." (Jeremiah 1:10, KJV)

Prayer: In the name of Jesus, this day I uproot, pull down, destroy and overthrow every diabolic seed, root or thing in my children (or child, name them), and plant the seed of God's word in their lives (decree God's word to/over them), and I plant my children in the house of the Lord. I decree and declare that my generation shall serve the Lord. In Jesus' name, I pray. Amen.

Rev. Dr. Mercy Forlu

Everyone needs compassion.

Be kind to one another, tenderhearted, forgiving one another, as God in Christ forgave you. (Ephesians 4:32 ESV)

The family unit is something that the enemy wants to attack and destroy. As believers and as leaders, when confronting family challenges, we must remember to always respond the way Christ responds to us. The response must be out of kindness, tenderness, and above all, forgiveness. Our families know us best, the leaders whom we surround ourselves with, and our church family know us well also. They know our triumphs, failures, and flaws. Because of this closeness, they can be the ones to hurt us the most with words and actions. Sometimes or most times, they do not even mean to hurt us. Thus, God's word encourages us to practice kindness, tenderness, and forgiveness. Many people struggle with forgiveness. But think about it this way: God, our Father, forgave us in all of our mess even when we hurt him with our words and turned our backs on him. So, shouldn't we be able to forgive our family members, fellow leaders, and church family for the things they do that may offend us? We are called to set the example. God wouldn't have called you to your position if he hadn't empowered you to handle things with love, grace, and mercy. Be encouraged today.

Prayer: Lord, help me to love, forgive and extend grace to those whom you have put into my life. In Jesus' name, I pray. Amen.

Pastor Angie Millar

Daily Devotions for the Pastor's Wife by PWANI

The pastor's wife's shoes are peace.

And, as shoes for your feet, having put on the readiness given by the gospel of peace. (Ephesians 6:15, ESV)

Her shoes—different colors, different brands, and different heights—all serve one function: to protect her feet and boost her posture. No matter how beautiful the shoes are if they do not fit, they become an impediment to their very function. They hurt your feet and distort your walk.

Your inner man has her own shoes, peace. We must protect our walk with God with our shoes of peace. If we will run the race to see the finish line, peace is not an option. Hebrews 12:14 says, "Strive for peace with everyone and work at living a holy life, for those who are not holy will not see the Lord." Peace is a security system that guards the treasures that God has deposited in your heart. Philippians 4:7 says, "And the peace of God which transcends all understanding will guard your heart and your minds in Christ Jesus."

Peace is not the absence of trouble but the presence of the *Prince of Peace*. Just as a river overcomes many obstacles on its way, but it never stops flowing, God has given us his peace as a river of life in our hearts (John 14:21). He knew that in this world, we would have trouble. The peace of God is not like the peace the world gives. The peace of God stems from an inner trust in the invisible presence of an Eternal Lover.

Prayer: Lord, grant me to daily, and in each moment, let the peace of Christ rule in my heart, since as members of one body I was called to peace. Help me to activate the rule of the peace of God in my heart by being thankful. (Colossians 3:15.) In Jesus' name, I pray. Amen.

Dr. Elizabeth Fondong

You have the power to swim gracefully—even in a fishbowl.

> ...We have been made a spectacle to the whole universe, to angels as well as to human beings. (1 Corinthians 4:9b, NIV)

Typically, fishbowls are clear. You can see the movements of the fish they contain. The fish swim, eat, and sleep while everyone watches. Sometimes, people watch in admiration. Other times, they watch out of pure curiosity, void of the care and concern of the fish owner. They are just curious about the color, movement, and life patterns of the fish.

Being a pastor's wife is a lot like being in a fishbowl. People observe you—not with the care and concern of your owner, the Lord—but out of pure curiosity. Paul could identify with this, saying that he felt he had been made a spectacle, not only to human beings but also to angels. Nevertheless, he goes on to say that, the kingdom of God is not in word, but in power. You see, those who are on display (spectacle) must tap into and abide in the power of the Holy Spirit. In the same way that a fish cannot survive without water, you and I cannot survive without cultivating the rivers of living water that come from the indwelling presence of the Holy Spirit.

I'm sure the fish is tempted to retreat when people touch the glass of the fishbowl or knock on it. But the fish is able to survive being a spectacle because, all the while, it remains in the water, its source of life. As long as we remain connected to Holy Spirit and rely on his power, we'll have what it takes to swim gracefully—even in a fishbowl. When you feel like all eyes are on you and you want to retreat, rely on the Holy Spirit's power; for, his strength is made perfect in weakness.

Prayer: Father, when all eyes are on me, help me to rely on the power of your Spirit. I declare that your grace is sufficient and by the power of your Spirit, I can fulfill my assignment as a pastor's wife with grace—even under spectacle. In Jesus' name, I pray. Amen.

Rev. Lenita Reeves

Do not defile the priesthood.

And one of the sons of Joiada, the son of Eliashib the high Priest, was son in law to Sanballat the Horonite: therefore I chased him from me. Remember them, O my God, because they have defiled the Priesthood, and the covenant of the Priesthood, and of the Levites. (Nehemiah 13: 28-29, KJV)

God has chosen our husbands as his priests; hence, he has set us apart unto himself. What a privilege. In Nehemiah chapter 13, the Jews were instructed not to intermarry with foreigners (the ungodly). Joiada, the son of Eliashib, the high priest, allowed his son to marry the daughter of Sanballat who was an enemy of God's people. Sanballat greatly fought against the building of the wall of Jerusalem. He did all he could to stop Nehemiah but failed. By so doing, Joiada's son defiled the priesthood. There was now a strange woman in that lineage. Her father's spirit of opposition was now practically present in the priesthood--to operate unhindered. Woman of God, we ought to pray earnestly to God that our children will not get married to the enemy of God, no matter how they disguise themselves. We cannot afford to defile the priesthood. Not all who appear godly are actually godly. The pain of marrying out of God's will is more painful than the pain of waiting on God for the right spouses for our children. May God help us.

Key Verse: "And you shall be holy unto me: for I the Lord am holy, and have severed you from other people, that ye should be mine." (Leviticus 20: 26, KJV)

Prayer: Dear Lord, help my children to be married to men and women whom you have chosen to be blessings, which will help preserve our priesthood. In Jesus' name, I pray. Amen.

Rev. Dr. Mercy Forlu.

Celebrate your uniqueness.

> *Having then gifts differing according to the grace that is given to us, let us use them: if prophecy, let us prophesy in proportion to our faith; or ministry, let us use it in our ministering; he who teaches, in teaching; he who exhorts, in exhortation; he who gives, with liberality; he who leads, with diligence; he who shows mercy, with cheerfulness. (Romans 12:6-8, New King James Version (NKJV))*

Growing up in church, it seemed every pastor's wife I knew played the piano or organ. Without fail, in each church we were invited to for a special service, you could find the pastor's wife perched behind a keyboard. Knowing in my heart, I was to be a pastor's wife, I began organ lessons at age 13 because I thought playing the piano or organ was a prerequisite for marrying a pastor and I wanted to be ready. I enjoyed learning; but, didn't love it. I admit, I mostly prayed for God to miraculously anoint me to play expertly without practicing and without the need to read music. After all, I did have an aunt who could beautifully play any instrument she picked up. Therefore, I thought "this runs in the family God, I have a head start" as I sat with my fingers hoovering over the keys. "Well," I thought to myself "if faith can move mountains… I'm about to play the keys right off this organ." Nothing happened. The Lord never miraculously bestowed upon me the gift of playing the organ and I am okay with that. He has given me other gifts to use for His glory, gifts unique for me, gifts that I have grown into, and am continuing to sharpen. He continues to show me new ways to use my gifts for my husband, my family, and his people.

I encourage you to celebrate and embrace your unique gifts and use them for his purpose. Wisely using everything we have to serve each other is part of fulfilling our purpose as God's set-apart people. Someone else's gifts were not designed for you. These differences are what make you special! Rather than wanting to change them, learn to embrace them.

Key Verse: "As each one has received a gift, minister it to one another, as good stewards of the manifold grace of God." (1 Peter 4:10, NKJV)

Prayer: Lord, help me to embrace my uniqueness. Help me to discover and use the gifts you have placed in me. In Jesus' name, I pray. Amen.

Pastor Angie Millar

Daily Devotions for the Pastor's Wife by PWANI

You're the only animal in this zoo.

> *And Adam gave names to all cattle, and to the fowl of the air, and to every beast of the field; but for Adam there was not found an help meet for him. (Genesis 2:20, KJV)*

> *So God created man in His own image, in the image and likeness of God He created him; male and female He created them. ²⁸ And God blessed them [granting them certain authority] and said to them, "Be fruitful, multiply, and fill the earth, and subjugate it [putting it under your power]; and rule over (dominate) the fish of the sea, the birds of the air, and every living thing that moves upon the earth." (Genesis 1:27-28, AMP)*

According to the Creation27 journal, Adam named approximately 2,500 proto-species of animals, birds, and livestock during creation. They estimate that it would have taken Adam three hours and 45 minutes to name them all, assuming he was naming them at a rate of one animal every five seconds. After he named the animals, birds, and livestock, God put him in a deep sleep and formed Eve from his side. Amazingly, even though Adam had never seen another human being, as soon as he saw Eve he exclaimed, "This is now bone of my bones and flesh of my flesh." Adam had been sleeping during the whole surgery and had never seen another human being; yet he knew Eve came out of him.

After naming 2,500 different types of animals, Adam understood that none of them was suitable to help him fulfill the one mandate he had been given—take dominion (Genesis 1:27-28). God blessed them—male and female—and told them both to dominate.

The *dominion mandate* is a *co-dominionship mandate*; meaning, you are the only animal designed, suited, and capable of joining your Adam—your husband—in the dominionship journey.

Adam exclaimed, "This is now bone of my bones and flesh of my flesh," because he realized that Eve was made of the same "stuff" he was made of. She was not like the other 2,500 animals he had named. She was the only animal suitable for the "zoo of life" called "taking dominion." Likewise, you are perfectly suited for the co-dominionship journey set before you as a pastor's wife. He placed that capacity in you at creation and blessed you to succeed in it. Rise up and take dominion!

Prayer: Lord, help me to dominate in life. Empower me for the task of *co-dominionship*. In Jesus' name, I pray. Amen.

Rev. Lenita Reeves

Daily Devotions for the Pastor's Wife by PWANI

You've been enlisted.

Let every soul be subject unto the higher powers. For there is no power but of God: the powers that be are ordained of God. (Romans 13:1)

In the United States, the Armed Forces are usually referred to as military service. Every day, there is a group of committed, trained, and dedicated soldiers ready to drop what they're doing to go fight wars, deliver supplies in territories, complete missions, and help in any crisis. They protect thousands of people they will never know. These armies consist of individuals who have laid down their opinions, differences, individualities, and lives for a country. They are not the original founders of the country. They are made up of everything that defines the word "different." That doesn't matter when their orders are given. They follow their Commander-in-Chief and all other members of appropriate authority. They ask no questions. They just follow the necessary protocols for which they have been trained. In the same manner, we follow God by the Holy Spirit and his example. We follow our spiritual leadership, trusting they have divine instructions, even if we don't understand. We are called to support, encourage, intercede, and protect our husband. He leads a mighty army for the Lord. We are the Lord's soldiers, and we have our orders. You have been trained and have chosen to lay your life down at the Cross to serve. Put your armor on; be ready.

Prayer: Father, I thank you for training, preparing and equipping me to serve you as I serve my husband and your children. In Jesus' name, I pray. Amen.

Pastor Angie Millar

There's grace to run the race.

But those who hope in the LORD will renew their strength. They will soar on wings like eagles; they will run and not grow weary, they will walk and not be faint. (Isaiah 40:31, NIV)

Do you ever feel like you're running a marathon and while running that marathon you're being pulled in 100 different directions? Sometimes life feels that way. You have a to-do list a mile long. And just when you think you're nearing the end, you remember something you forgot. As women, we tend to go 100 miles per hour without stopping. We're always going. Some of us are a model for the saying, "If you want something done, do it yourself."

Don't grow weary doing the Lord's work. Don't get weary completing that mile-long list of never-ending responsibilities. You may be doing the work without recognition. The race will soon end. The prize you will receive will be greater than any you could've ever imagined.

Prayer: Lord, help me to run this race with patience. Help me to remember that you are a rewarder of those who remain diligent in seeking you. In Jesus' name, I pray. Amen.

Mrs. Danyel Forlu

About the Authors

Pastor Mercy Forlu

Pastor Mercy Forlu was born in Ekona-Yard, Southwest Region, Cameroon, to Moses and Rebecca Tangi on the 18th day of July 1960. Pastor Mercy began her walk with the Lord in 1978. At the time, she was the only one in both her immediate and extended family who had surrendered her life to Christ. She suffered many persecutions and was rejected by her relatives when an emergency family gathering was summoned to discuss her decision to walk with Jesus. Thank God that, despite the hard persecutions she suffered, she stood for Jesus, uncompromisingly, and has been faithfully serving Him in numerous capacities since.

Pastor Mercy is a nurse by profession. She began her career in this prestigious and noble profession back in Cameroon in 1981 as a Licensed Practical Nurse. She later went on to advance her career and graduated as a Registered Nurse in1987. She has since worked in various capacities in the nursing industry, including:
 - Registered Nurse at Holy Cross Hospital, Silver Spring, Maryland, United States
 - CEO / Founder, and Director of Nursing at Grace and Mercy Health Services, founded in 2002. Serving patients and persons with intellectual disability in Maryland and Washington DC respectively.
 - CEO / Founder, of Grace and Mercy Community Services, founded 2016. Both companies where founded in the United States, where she still sits in the respective positions.

As vast as Pastor Mercy's accomplishments are in the healthcare field, they are even vaster in the work she does to further the kingdom of God. For the past 37 years, Pastor Mercy has served alongside her husband, Bishop Dr. Israel Forlu, in preaching the gospel. They began their ministry work under the umbrella of the Full Gospel Mission in Cameroon. In the year 2000, they relocated to the United States of America, where they both found the River of Life Assemblies International (ROLAI) in 2002.

During her time with the Full Gospel Mission, Cameroon, Pastor Mercy was privileged to serve in the following capacities:
Pastor Mercy served as
- District Women's Leader from 1988 to 1995,
- Vice National Women's Leader from 1996 to 2000.

As the District Women's Leader, Pastor Mercy organized women's retreats and conferences. She also focused on empowering women in the areas of Godly leadership, living Godly lives, and how to have a successful marriage. In 1989, by Divine inspiration, she was led by the Holy Spirit to launch an intercessory prayer warrior's team. To date, she continues in her capacity as a Visionary, Watchman, Prophetic Prayer Warrior, and Intercessor at the ROLAI.

.In 1998, she obtained a diploma in Biblical Studies in the South West Bible Training Institude Limbe Cameroon. In 1999, Pastor Mercy founded the Women for Jesus ministry when she organized a deliverance march for Cameroon, in the city of Limbe, in the South West Region of Cameroon. After an encounter with God, Pastor Mercy was instructed to gather women from various churches together to march against that proclamation. All the women wore t-shirts with the inscription "Women for Jesus," on the front; and appropriately the back of the t-shirts read "Jesus Christ King of Cameroon" and they marched in the city of Limbe. There were approximately 2,000 women who participated in the march. During the march, the women processed with banners for Christ and possessed the land for King Jesus. Along with women, the Limbe Council of Clergy and government officials gathered at the end of the march at the Limbe stadium to repent on behalf of the nation and declare Jesus Christ as King of the nation. The event was truly remarkable and Holy Spirit inspired. To this day, the Women for Jesus ministry still wears "Women for Jesus" t-shirts during their community outreach events, such as feed the hungry, evangelism, and during their women for Jesus marches that take place during their annual conferences in Maryland, USA,

In 2002, Pastor Mercy assisted her husband, Bishop Dr. Israel Forlu in founding the River of Life Center, which later became the River of Life Assemblies International (ROLAI). She was later ordained to the office of Pastor and is licensed to function in that capacity. They currently serve as the presiding bishop and pastor of all ROLAI branches. The ministry began 16 years ago in the basement of their home and has grown to include branches across the United States.

In 2013, Pastor Mercy founded the Teens for Jesus ministry, which is overseen by her daughter, Grace. In 2014, Pastor Mercy founded the Pastors' Wives Arise Network International (PWANI). PWANI is a multi-denominational network that brings together Pastors' wives from various churches around the globe, to empower them so that they may be of positive influence in their homes, churches, and communities. Each year PWANI holds their annual international conference in Maryland, USA, where Pastors' wives from around the world attend.

She has an honorary Doctorate of Divinity, awarded by Cornerstone University and Theological Seminary Owerri, Nigeria. Pastor Mercy is a Certified Public Speaker by the John Maxwell Team, and a candidate for a degree in Pastoral Leadership from Newburgh Theological Seminary, Indiana. Rev. Dr. Mercy is married to Bishop Dr. Israel Forlu for 37 years and counting; and they are blessed with five Godly children who are all ministers of the Gospel. They're also blessed with three exquisitely gorgeous daughters-in-love and eight grandchildren. To God Almighty be all the glory in Jesus' name.

Dr. Elizabeth Fondong

Dr. Elizabeth Fondong is multi-gifted international conference speaker, a dynamic servant of God, medical doctor, wellness consultant and marriage counselor.

She is the founder of *Arise and Shine Women's Ministries* under Christian Missionary Fellowship International Maryland. She founded Hope Natural and Wellness Center and The Shepherd Health Revolution; A ministry of health and wellness to pastors and pastoral families.

She and her husband Pastor Robinson are blessed with 3 boys. They travel around the world preaching the gospel of the kingdom and setting men free.

Danyel Forlu

Danyel Forlu serves alongside her husband at the River of Life Assemblies International where he is the assistant pastor. Mrs. Forlu is the director of the Kids' For Jesus Ministry and she and her husband have four beautiful children, Samuel, Daniel, Mercy, and Grace. She has a bachelor's degree in Elementary and Special Education and enjoys life as a stay-at-home mom.

Pastor Angie Millar

Pastor Angie Millar serves alongside her husband as the assistant pastors at Terre Haute Church of God in Terre Haute, IN, where they have served as assistant pastors for almost 15 years. Pastor Angie has been married to the love of her life for 29 years and they have 3 children and 10 grandchildren. She works at the Crisis Pregnancy Center as an LPN and counselor.

Pastor Lenita Reeves

Rev. Lenita Reeves is the senior pastor of Action Chapel Baltimore, a prophetic church under the covering of Archbishop Nicholas Duncan-Williams, who ordained her into ministry and the founder of PurposeHouse Counseling and PurposeHouse Publishing.

She is the author of several books including, *I Am: The Divine Purpose Manifesto* and *Fervent Fire: Understanding the pattern of the priesthood for prevailing intercessory prayer*.

As a rape survivor and former teen mom, God has graced Lenita to be an outspoken overcomer, sharing her testimony freely and as a result, seeing captives set free all over the world. A featured conference speaker, she is a member of the RAINN speaker's bureau. She has traveled the world to conduct apostolic missions and train leaders in London, Jamaica, Haiti, the Bahamas, Kenya, Uganda and Ghana.

She began her service to the Lord in campus ministry. As Deputy Director of Campus Ministries United, she assisted in planting campus branches and in the coordination of an annual conference aimed at bringing various campus groups together in a night of prayer, praise, and relationship building. In the next phase of her ministry, God taught her the basics of pastoring while serving as a youth minister.

Some call her preacher and some call her teacher, but all agree that she is a prolific voice who speaks with transparency, highlighting her highs as well as her lows to show others that God can turn pain into a platform and use the foolish things of this world to confound the wise.

From senior class president to director in Corporate America to founder of a non-profit and pastor, leadership has been an evident mark of Lenita's calling and passions throughout her life. She has a Bachelor of Science in Industrial Engineering from Georgia Tech, a Master of Arts in Dance Education from the Ohio State University and a MBA from the University of Maryland, College Park. She is currently a doctoral candidate in Christian Counseling and attended Beulah Heights University in Atlanta, Georgia, which was then under the leadership of Dr. Sam Chand.

Pastor Lenita was ordained in Action Chapel International in Ghana under the leadership of Archbishop Nicholas Duncan-Williams and Action Chapel North America under the leadership of Bishop Kibby Otoo. She is married to Pastor Cephas Reeves and they have four children, Elijah, Cenita, Ethan and Joshua.

In addition to her books, her speaking topics include:
- Leadership Development
    - Discovering Your Personal Leadership
    - "Followship": Bearing the Burden with Senior Leadership
    - MED School © Ministers, Elders and Deacon Leadership School
    - Women in Leadership
- Understanding the Purpose of the Marriage Bed
- Journey to Redemption: Healing from Abuse
- New Testament Priesthood and Intercession

For more information about Pastor Lenita, visit www.purposehose.net or www.facebook.com/pastorlenita.

www.ingramcontent.com/pod-product-compliance
Lightning Source LLC
Chambersburg PA
CBHW071731040426
42446CB00011B/2315